WHALES and DOLPHINS

by
Anton Ericson

Scientific Consultant:
Lisa Mielke
Education Department
New York Aquarium

Kidsbooks®

Copyright © 1999, 2008, Kidsbooks, LLC
3535 West Peterson Avenue
Chicago, IL 60659

Printed in China
0109-02-005

Visit us at www.kidsbooks.com®

CONTENTS

LIVING LARGE

Spotted dolphins

It's amazing, but true. Some whales are even larger than the biggest dinosaurs were. Whales have lived on Earth for about 50 million years. As their food supply increased, whales ate more and became bigger over time. The blue whale is the largest animal that has ever lived. It can grow to 100 feet long and weigh about 300,000 pounds. That's as heavy as 25 elephants!

This baby humpback whale, swimming with its mother, might grow as long as 60 feet as an adult and weigh as much as 40 tons. ▶

FAST AND FUN ▲

When you think of dolphins, you probably think of fun. You're right! These speedsters are very playful. Ranging from about six feet to 13 feet long, dolphins like to leap clear out of the water and ride the waves made by boats.

Gray whale showing baleen in upper jaw.

6

TOOTH OR COMB

Cetaceans are grouped according to how they eat. Some have teeth that snag sea creatures. Others, like the big gray whale (left), have comblike structures called baleen. With baleen, whales can filter the sea for food and eat thousands of pounds every day. No wonder they grow to such enormous sizes!

Dolphin with teeth

SOUNDS FISHY

Although they live in water, whales and dolphins are not fish. They are mammals. Like humans, they are warm-blooded. A thick layer of fat, called blubber, helps them keep warm and survive in cold water. Also, cetaceans have lungs rather than gills. They breathe through a blowhole at the top of their head. And, they don't hatch eggs, but give birth to their babies and then nurse them on milk.

◀ This fin whale exhales from its blowhole.

Dall's porpoise

WATER PIGLETS

The porpoise probably gets its name, which means "pig-fish" in Latin, from being so short and chubby. Ranging from 4 to 7 feet long, most porpoises aren't as playful or as fast as dolphins. However, the Dall's porpoise is known for zipping through the water and kicking up white spray.

TOTALLY TOOTHED

The majority of whales, including all dolphins and porpoises, have teeth. But they don't chew. They swallow their food whole. In fact, most toothed whales only use their teeth to catch and hold their prey.

▲ Dusky dolphins enjoying a meal of anchovies.

◄ Common dolphins are very energetic swimmers, which helps them catch the 10 to 20 pounds of food they eat each day.

THE UNICORN LOOK

It may seem incredible, but the long spear on the head of narwhals is actually a tooth. Narwhals have two teeth, but in the males, the one on the left side grows through the upper lip and reaches up to 10 feet long. Scientists believe that it's used to attract females. Whatever its purpose, this fantastic tusk gives the narwhal the look of a swimming unicorn.

WHITE WHALE ▶

Beluga whales favor shallow, coastal waters and use suction to capture prey. They suck in fish, squid, crabs, shrimp, clams, and worms.

ZAP AND TRAP ▼

Experts believe that the sperm whale produces sound waves from its large head, which stun the giant 400-pound squid living in the ocean depths. The whale then swallows its favorite food whole.

WHALE HUNGRY ▼

Killer whales definitely use their 50 cone-shaped teeth to grab. Also known as *orcas*, a name that comes from Orcus, the Roman god of the underworld, these killers can cut a seal in half. Traveling in packs, they will attack not only fish, but also big baleen whales, dolphins, porpoises, turtles, and penguins.

FANG FIGHTS

The male sperm whale uses his teeth to fight other males during mating season. The 24 to 30 cone-shaped teeth on each side of the lower jaw grow up to seven inches long and weigh as much as two pounds each.

This sperm whale tooth was scrimshawed, or engraved, in 1877 by whalers.

FILTER FEEDERS

It may seem odd, but there are 10 kinds of whales that don't have any teeth at all. Hanging from their upper jaws are rows of bristled strands called baleen. Made of a material similar to the human fingernail, the baleen acts as a food filter.

Baleen

▲ A humpback whale feeding (note baleen).

SQUEEZE PLAY

Baleen whales eat by taking in a mouthful of water and then "spitting" it out. Anything too large to squeeze through the baleen, such as krill, anchovies, sardines, and herring, is left behind to be swallowed.

KRILL-A-PLENTY

Many baleen whales feed on krill—orange sea creatures that look like shrimp and grow up to two inches long. Scientists estimate that there may be six and a half billion tons in the Antarctic Ocean alone! A blue whale eats four tons of krill every day.

SUPER SCOOPERS

Gray whales do not gulp their food. Living close to the shore in the Pacific Ocean, they swim to the bottom of the sea and lie on their side. There they scoop up a mouthful of mud and then force it back out through their baleen. What's left behind is a dinner of crabs and clams.

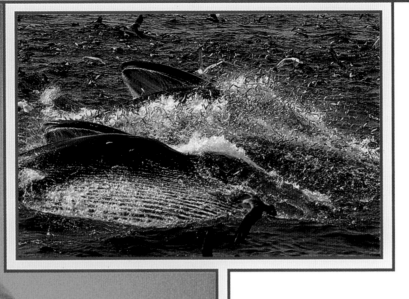

GULPING GOODIES

Fin whales, as well as blue, Bryde's, humpback, sei, and minke whales, are specially equipped to take huge gulps of krill and fish at one time. On their throats, there are grooves, or pleats, that stretch to allow the throat to expand.

◀ Fin whales feeding on a school of herring.

▼ A humpback's bubble net.

BUBBLE TROUBLE

Because humpback whales prefer fish to krill, they sometimes eat in a special way, called bubble-net feeding. The humpback blows air from its blowhole as it swims in a spiral below a school of fish. The bubbles rise in a "net," surrounding the frightened fish. The whale then swims inside the net of bubbles, catching the trapped fish.

▲ Humpback whales also feed by *lunging* into a school of fish that they've herded into a ball.

THE TALE OF TAILS

Whales and dolphins propel themselves through the water with their tails, which have two strong wings, or *flukes.* Instead of wagging their flukes from side to side like fish, they move them up and down in powerful strokes.

A sperm whale's huge, triangular ▶ flukes are 13 feet across.

The blue whale's 16-foot flukes ▶ are relatively small for such an enormous animal.

Humpbacks raise their flukes when diving. ▼

a breeding program for the few black-footed ferrets remaining.

Maned wolf Maned wolves live on the dry, grassy plains of some South American countries. They look like red dogs on stilts, and although they are as big as wolves and are called wolves, they are really a type of fox. Maned wolves can travel distances of 20 miles (30 km) a night, and they hunt rabbits, mice, and other rodents, as well as birds.

Flying fox Bats make up nearly one-quarter of all the mammals that exist. Of these, there are 173 different kinds of flying fox. In Malaysia and Indonesia bats are hunted for their meat, which is thought to be a delicacy. Some people mistakenly believe that bat meat will cure asthma. A hunter with a modern shotgun can wipe out a colony of a thousand flying foxes in a short time.

Flying foxes are disappearing from many places where their treetop homes are being cut down for firewood or to clear land for agriculture. In the United States, Bat Conservation International is trying to spread the word about the need to preserve and nurture the Earth's bat population and stop any more species from being wiped out.

Merlin D. Tuttle/Bat Conservation International

▲ Many flying foxes, like this Marianas fruit bat, are seriously endangered because humans destroy their habitat.

Francisco Erize/Bruce Coleman Limited

◀ The maned wolf of South America is hunted by collectors for zoos and by local people for its supposed magical properties. There are fewer than 2,000 left in the wild.

A venomous Australian

The platypus is one of a very few venomous mammals. All three species of monotreme have spurs on their rear ankles. But the spur of the male platypus is the only one that can inject venom. Adult males have spurs about ½ inch (15 mm) long. The puncture the spur can make is painful enough, but the venom can cause swelling and paralysis in a human limb and has been know to kill dogs. No one knows exactly what the spurs or their venom are for.

venom gland

venom duct

spur

Platypuses and Echidnas

There are three species of monotreme alive today: the duck-billed platypus, the long-beaked echidna, and the short-beaked echidna. Both species of echidna are found in New Guinea, and the short-beaked echidna and platypus are found in Australia. Neither they nor their fossils have been found anywhere else in the world.

Egg-laying mammals

Monotremes are mammals that lay eggs instead of giving birth to live young. The word "monotreme" means "one hole." This refers to the fact that monotremes have only one opening to the outside of the body, through which they both lay eggs and excrete waste products. The eggs that monotremes lay have leathery

▼ The platypus swims by using alternate kicks of its webbed front feet. All other amphibious mammals kick with the hind limbs.

shells. The mothers incubate them for 10 days before the eggs hatch, and then suckle the young with their milk.

Duck-billed platypus

The duck-billed platypus is one of the strangest looking mammals. When a platypus corpse was sent back to Britain in 1798 it was assumed to be a fake, made by stitching the beak of a duck onto the body of a mammal!

The platypus is about half the size of a domestic cat. It is amphibious (adapted to live in water as well as on

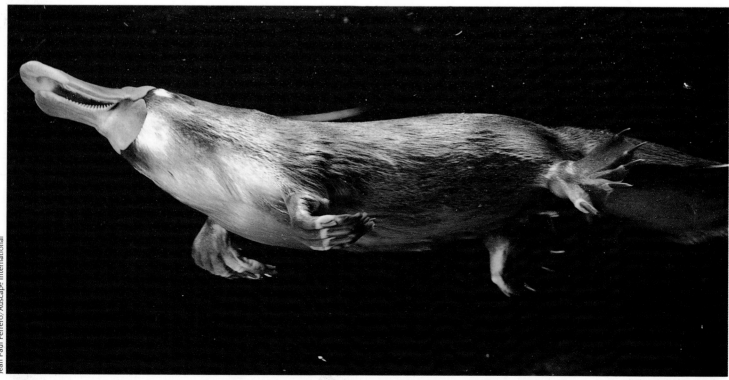

land) and feeds mostly at night, in the streams, rivers, and lakes of eastern Australia. It dives for the larvae (young) of small insects and for other invertebrates (animals without backbones). Its ears and eyes are housed in a groove that closes when the platypus is underwater. The platypus finds food with its soft, rubbery bill, which has many nerve endings and is very sensitive. Food is collected in cheek pouches, and between dives the platypus spends a few minutes chewing its prey between the horny pads that replace the teeth in adults.

Platypuses live in burrows, which they dig in riverbanks. The platypus can keep the temperature of its body steady at 90°F (32°C) even when it swims for long spells in near-freezing water.

Echidnas

Both species of echidna (also called spiny anteaters) have long beak-like snouts, no teeth, long sticky tongues, and sharp spines on their backs and sides. Short-beaked echidnas, at 11 to 18 inches (30 to 45 cm) long, are much smaller than the long-beaked species.

The short-beaked echidna eats termites, ants, and insect larvae. It digs into the mounds and nests of these insects with its large front claws and

 (vertical caption) D. Parer & E. Parer-Cook/Auscape International

then picks up the ants and termites with its sticky tongue.

The female short-beaked echidna grows a pouch during the breeding season and lays one egg in it. After about 10 days the baby hatches and drinks milk from the milk patches in the pouch. When the young begins to grow spines (at around 9 weeks) it is left in a burrow; the mother returns to feed it.

An adult long-beaked echidna is 18 to 35 inches (45 to 90 cm) long and weighs 11 to 22 pounds (5 to 10 kg). The long-beaked echidna has more hair and fewer spines than its short-beaked relative.

▲ *The long-beaked echidna eats mainly worms. It uses spines in a groove in its tongue to draw worms into its mouth. Its nostrils and mouth are at the end of the beak.*

D. Parer & E. Parer-Cook/Auscape International

▲ *The short-beaked echidna can push its snout into small spaces, then stretch out its long sticky tongue into even smaller spaces to reach its insect food.*

◄ *Mother and baby short-beaked echidnas. When they are frightened, echidnas dig straight down into the ground until you can see only the tips of their spines. Dingos are one of the few predators able to dig them out and eat them, spines and all.*

D. Parer & E. Parer-Cook/Auscape International

Small Marsupials

Marsupials give birth to live young that are not fully developed. The young are suckled in a pouch on their mother's belly until they develop fully. Marsupials — about 275 species altogether — can be divided into two groups: those that live in North, Central, and South America and those that live in Australia, New Guinea, and nearby islands.

▲ Only one species of numbat survives today in southwestern Australia. With its long, sticky tongue, this squirrel-size marsupial feeds almost entirely on ants and termites.

▼ The Tasmanian devil is the marsupial equivalent of the hyena. While it does catch some live prey, it mainly scavenges food that has been killed by other animals.

American marsupials

There are about seventy-five species of American marsupial, all of which are called opossums. These are divided into three family groups: American opossums, shrew opossums, and the colocolo or monito del monte.

American opossums are "true" opossums. They range in size from one species about as small as a mouse to the cat-size Virginian opossum. Most are omnivores (animals that eat both animal and plant foods) and are able to climb. Those that spend more time on the ground than in trees have shorter tails and eat more meat than the tree opossums. Opossums are not afraid to live near humans and sometimes become pests in orchards.

The yapok, or water opossum, is the only truly amphibious marsupial, living half its life in water and half on land. The female gives birth to 5 or 6 young. By tightening her muscles she makes her pouch watertight and can take her babies swimming with her as she hunts for food in freshwater lakes and streams.

The seven species of shrew opossum live in the cool, misty forests of the Andes Mountains in South America. They are the size of mice or rats. Two long incisors (cutting teeth) stick forward from their bottom jaw and are used to stab the large insects and small animals upon which they prey.

The colocolo, or monito del monte ("little monkey of the mountain"), lives in the cool rain forests of southern Chile in South America. Natives of the Lake Region of Chile believe that seeing this rat-size opossum brings bad luck.

Small Australian marsupials

There are about 200 species of Australian marsupial. They can be divided into four groups: the carnivorous marsupials (meat-eaters); the marsupial mole; the bandicoot group; and the large group of diprotodonts, which includes koalas, wombats, possums, and kangaroos.

Meat-eating marsupials The three families of meat-eating marsupials have three or four pairs of narrow, pointed incisors on their upper jaw and three pairs on their lower jaw. Their hind feet have four or five toes. The Tasmanian devil, the Tasmanian tiger, and the numbat belong to this group.

Bandicoots All bandicoots are omnivores. Small species are rat-size, and larger species are as big as badgers. They are well known — in fact, notorious

David Kirshner

— as carriers of ticks. Bandicoots use their strong front claws to burrow for insects, larvae, and the succulent parts of plants that grow underground.

Diprodonts More than half of all Australian marsupials belong to this

▲ *The woolly opossum (top) has an extremely long tail — at about 20 inches (50 cm) it is twice as long as its head and body. The yapok, or water opossum (bottom), has webbed back feet that paddle with a running motion. Because its eyes are shut tight while it is under the water, the yapok feels for soft animals at the bottom of freshwater lakes and streams with its sensitive fingers.*

Tiger or wolf?

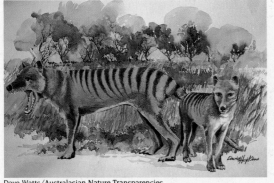

Dave Watts/Australasian Nature Transparencies

The thylacine, or "Tasmanian tiger," probably died out in the 1930s. This meat-eating marsupial was more than 3 feet (1 m) long from its head to the end of its body. Except for its stripes, it looked more like a wolf than a tiger. Because it sometimes attacked sheep, the thylacine was hunted in its native Tasmania — an island off the south coast of Australia — and the last known individual died in a zoo in 1933.

David Kirshner

▲ *The squirrel glider (top left) has a membrane that stretches from its ankle to its wrist. The striped possum (top right) digs into the tunnels of wood-boring insects with its sharp teeth and pulls the insects out with its long fourth finger. Cuscuses (bottom) have powerfully prehensile tails.*

▶ *"Koala" is said to be an Australian Aboriginal word meaning "doesn't drink," but it is more likely to mean "biter." Koalas are very aggressive toward each other and can defend themselves against dogs and humans by biting and scratching.*

J. Cancalosi/Auscape International

group of mammals. They have only one pair of well-developed incisors in their lower jaw.

The three living species of wombat belong to the diprodont group. They look like miniature bears, but are very timid and eat only grass. From fossils scientists have discovered that Australia was once home to a species of giant wombat the size of a hippopotamus.

Wombats are nocturnal and live in huge burrows, some up to 100 feet (30 m) long.

The koala is a distant relative of the wombat. It has long arms and legs and almost no tail, and for its size it has a remarkably small brain.

Cuscuses and the scaly-tailed possum have strongly prehensile tails. The brushtail possum is the most common type of possum found in Australia.

Ringtails possums are so called because of their long, slender, prehensile tails, which they carry tightly curled when not in use. All species except the rock ringtail live in trees.

The cat-size greater glider has a membrane that stretches between the elbow and ankle on each side of its body. It uses this as a parachute to glide from tree to tree. The greater glider has been recorded traveling distances of over 300 feet (100 m) in this way.

The smallest diprodonts are the five species of pygmy possum, which weigh a mere ¼ to 1½ ounces (7 to 40 g). Four species live in trees and eat nectar, pollen, and insects. The fifth species, the mountain pygmy possum, lives mainly on the ground and feeds on plants, seeds, and insects.

▶ *The tiny feathertail glider is only 3 inches (8 cm) long — smaller than any other mammal that glides. Its feather-like tail helps to steer it over flights of 65 feet (20 m).*

Jean Paul Ferrero/Auscape International

The mysterious marsupial mole

The marsupial mole is the only living member of its family. Very little is known of its behavior, although we know that all moles must feed continuously because of the amount of energy they use in burrowing. After eating they fall asleep. When they awake, they immediately begin their frantic search for food again.

The Australian marsupial mole and the golden moles of Africa are remarkably similar and are a good example of convergent evolution (where two different animals in different parts of the world evolve to become almost identical).

M.W. Gillam/Auscape International

▲ *The marsupial mole feeds on burrowing insects and reptiles. It does not make a tunnel but "swims" through the sand, which collapses behind it. It breathes oxygen from the air trapped between the grains of sand.*

▶ The musky rat-kangaroo is only 9 inches (23 cm) long. It has five toes on its back feet instead of four like other kangaroos, and its tail is prehensile. It is the only kangaroo to have twins rather than just one baby at a time.

David Kirshner

The five species of rat-kangaroo are more primitive than kangaroos but are descended from the same ancestors. One species, the musky rat-kangaroo, has a four-legged hop; all four feet touch the ground at the same time. It has never been seen hopping on two legs like its larger kangaroo relatives.

Other members of this family are potoroos and bettongs. Most of these marsupials feed on the underground stems of plants, bulbs, and fungi such as mushrooms and molds, as well as plants. They use their tails to balance while hopping and also for carrying nesting materials.

Jean-Paul Ferrero/Auscape International

▲ The tiny honey possum eats only nectar. Its long, brush-tipped tongue enables it to extract nectar from the wildflowers of southwestern Australia.

Pouch pups

Marsupial babies grow quickly inside their mother's uterus (womb). The tiny newborn babies drag themselves up their mother's fur, into the pouch, and attach themselves to a teat. They all look alike. Their skin is bare, thin, and richly supplied with blood; their ears and eyes are still undeveloped; and their hind limbs are short, with buds where the toes will grow. But their nostrils are huge, and their sense of smell is well developed. Their forelimbs are large in relation to the rest of their bodies and have powerful, needle-sharp claws.

Jean Paul Ferrero/Auscape International

▲ This red kangaroo baby is more than a month old. Although it is still blind and hairless, it now has hind limbs and a tail.

Hans & Judy Beste/Auscape International

Dave Watts/Australasian Nature Transparencies

▲ The dunnart is a member of the diprodont group of marsupials. This fierce little hunter, the size of a house mouse, hunts prey almost as big as itself. This one is eating a desert grasshopper. Females carrying young in their pouch will attack males and even kill their mates.

◄ Wombats look like small bears, but they are very timid and eat only grass. They dig huge tunnel systems and emerge mostly at night.

Anteaters, Armadillos, and Sloths

Anteaters, armadillos, and sloths are all known as edentates. "Edentate" is the Latin word for "without teeth." But of these three animals, it is really only the anteater that has no teeth at all. The sloth and the armadillo have molars (large grinding teeth) with no roots, which grow continuously during the animal's life.

▼ *The huge claws and strong front legs of the giant anteater are good for digging into rock-hard termite mounds. Its long, worm-like tongue, covered with sticky saliva, laps up to 35,000 insects per day.*

Edentates originated in North America and traveled across the land bridge to South America many millions of years ago. Then the land bridge between the two American continents became submerged below sea level. For some 70 million years the South American land mass was isolated. During this time the animals there evolved into some of the most bizarre species alive today.

Anteaters were probably one of the first groups of mammals to reach South America before it became an island.

Giant anteaters

The giant anteater is gray with a black and white shoulder stripe. Despite its name, it isn't a huge animal. The giant anteater grows to about 4 feet (110 cm) in length. It lives on the grasslands and in the open woodlands of South America, but sometimes goes into the rain forests looking for ants and termites, its favorite foods. The giant anteater's sense of smell is forty times more sensitive than that of humans, and it uses its elongated snout to sniff the air for food.

Although the giant anteater can climb trees, it is usually found on the ground. It walks on its knuckles with its two largest claws turned inward. These claws make it harder for the animal to walk, but they make very good weapons. The anteater stands up on its back legs and slashes and rips at its enemies. Jaguars — powerful wild cats — avoid fighting with the giant anteater.

Tamanduas and silky anteaters

The collared anteater, or tamandua, and the two-toed, or silky, anteater live in dense forests and woodlands of central and northern South America. They live in trees and do not often come down to the ground, where they might be attacked. Tamanduas have smooth fawn fur and are about half the size of giant anteaters. Their hairless tails are prehensile. Tamanduas sleep during the day and are active at night.

Silky anteaters are even smaller and shyer than tamanduas. They are also active at night, and they spend all of their lives in the treetops. They don't eat termites but prefer the ants that live on lianas and tree branches. Their snouts are not as long as those of their relatives, but their tongues are similarly long and sticky. Their fur is long, yellow, and silky, and their tails are longer than their bodies.

Even though silky anteaters live in

trees, they are not safe from all enemies. Eagles and owls attack them from the air. When this happens, the anteaters rear up on their back legs and slash with their claws.

▲ *The silky anteater often feeds by carrying food to its mouth with its huge front claws after moistening its hands with saliva.*

Michael Fodgen/Oxford Scientific Films

▶ The sloth leaves the trees only to empty its bowels, about once a week. The three-toed sloth is so adapted to hanging upside-down that it has lost the ability to stand upright and must drag itself along the ground by its forearms.

Joe McDonald/Tom Stack & Associates

Francisco Erize/Bruce Coleman Limited

▲ When threatened, the three-banded armadillo rolls itself into a ball, leaving a small gap between the edges of its curled shell. If a predator pokes its nose or paw into this gap, the armadillo snaps its shell shut like a steel trap.

Sloths

There are two families of sloth — the three-toed sloth and the two-toed sloth. Both families live in the tropical rain forests of Central and South America.

Sloths are herbivores. Most of their diet is made up of leaves, because they live most of their lives in trees. They only come down to the ground about once a week to empty waste matter from their bowels. In fact, sloths are so good at moving about in trees that they have almost lost the ability to walk

Gary Milburn/Tom Stack & Associates

The world turned upside-down

Sloths sleep up to 18 hours a day and spend most of their lives hanging upside-down in the treetops. They are so well adapted to this position that they eat, sleep, mate, and give birth upside-down! When they move, they do so extremely slowly and deliberately. Sloths in trees look like large, furry coat hangers.

◀ The two-toed sloth lives in mountain rain forests. While awake, it feeds almost continuously on leaves.

along on the ground.

The sloth is covered with a dense, soft fleece with tufts of longer, coarser hair sticking through. These hairs have grooves in them where tiny green algae grow. When it rains the sloth gets wet, the algae multiply, and the sloth's hairs become green. This helps to camouflage these mammals from enemies such as eagles and jaguars.

Armadillos

Spanish explorers were the first Europeans to see armadillos and gave the animal its name. It means "little armored thing." The armor of the armadillo is a flexible horny shield. This body shell grows from the skin and is made of strong, bony plates with a covering of horn. The belly is covered by a soft, hairy skin.

Most armadillos live in deep underground tunnels in desert areas with little vegetation. They spend their days curled up asleep and come out at night.

The armadillo eats ants, termites, and a variety of other insects. It also eats small vertebrates (animals with

backbones) and plants. The giant armadillo, the same size as the giant anteater, habitually digs a tunnel right into the center of a termite mound and doesn't seem to notice the bites of the several thousand angry termites it disturbs on its way.

When in danger, most armadillos run, or dig a burrow very quickly. Some species block the entrance to their burrow with the tough armor of their rear end. Only one species, the three-banded armadillo, does not burrow: it rolls itself up into a tight ball.

Will edentates survive?

The lives of many sloths, anteaters, and armadillos are under threat. Some of these mammals, such as the giant anteater, are hunted as trophies. Others have lost their homes — grasslands have been stocked with thousands of cattle, which eat the grasses, and rain forests are being destroyed by logging. The survival of these unusual creatures depends on humans. If we do not make an effort to protect them, they are almost certainly doomed.

▼ *Like all species of armadillo, this Patagonian armadillo has a very sensitive sense of smell. It can detect insects, worms, and snails 8 inches (20 cm) underground.*

Francisco Erize/Bruce Coleman Limited

S.C. Bisserot

▲ The hedgehog tenrec really does look like a "true" hedgehog, but it is found only on the island of Madagascar.

▼ The streaked tenrec from Madagascar has barbed spines loosely attached to its neck. If the animal is attacked these spines become stuck in the skin of the aggressor.

David Kirshner

Insect-eaters

The order of insectivores (insect-eaters) is an ancient one. It was probably from their ancestors that most modern mammals evolved. Most insectivores are small, highly mobile, and have long, narrow snouts. With more than 400 species, insectivores are the third-largest group of mammals.

Insectivores live in North America, Canada, Europe, the Soviet Union, Africa, and in southern Asia. Their brains are not very well developed, and they depend more on their sense of smell than on vision.

Solenodons

Solenodons are among the largest of the insectivores alive today. They measure about 12 inches (30 cm) in length, and their tails are nearly as long again. They can be found only on Cuba and Hispaniola, two islands in the Caribbean Sea. They are in great danger of becoming extinct. Introduced animals such as dogs, rats, and mongooses have either killed the solenodons or competed for their food.

A solenodon sleeps during the day and comes out to feed at night. It has a small brain, but a highly developed sense of touch. It uses its snout like a tentacle to search for food in cracks and its strong claws to break up rotting vegetation.

Solenodons also eat meat, which is unusual for an insectivore. Once it finds prey, the solenodon bites it quickly and injects a small amount of poisonous saliva into the victim, causing paralysis.

The female solenodon gives birth to 1 baby at a time in a special nesting burrow.

Tenrecs and otter shrews

The tenrecs of Madagascar and the otter shrews of Central Africa look, and act, rather like hedgehogs. Fossils show that members of this family were established in Africa more than 25 million years ago. The only members of this ancient family to inhabit mainland Africa today are three species of otter shrew.

Tenrecs were among the first mammals to arrive on the island of Madagascar after its separation from mainland Africa about 150 million years ago. They are small animals — the largest weighs 2 pounds (1 kg) and the smallest less than ²⁄₅ ounce (10 g). Tenrecs are active at twilight or at night.

Golden moles

The golden mole of Africa gets its name from the shiny bronze tint on its fur. The golden mole's body is thick and strong: it can exert a force 150 times its own weight. Its front legs are powerful and are armed with four short digging claws.

Golden moles are solitary animals. Some species spend 75 percent of their waking hours burrowing. Desert-living golden moles do not form lasting burrows but push their way through the

sand with a "swimming" action. These desert moles occasionally hunt legless lizards and insects on top of the sand.

Hedgehogs

Hedgehogs live in parts of Europe, Africa, and Asia. Some have also been introduced to New Zealand. During the summer months they build a simple nest from leaves and grasses. These are usually placed at the bottom of trees where there are plants growing to give protection. In winter they take more care where they build their nests, as it is important that they keep out the cold.

Hedgehogs, like other insectivores, use up a great deal of energy looking for food. When the weather is very cold, or food is scarce, they hibernate (stop being active) in order to store their

▲ This strange insectivore eats meat. The solenodon bites its prey and injects its victim with a poisonous saliva, causing paralysis.

▼ The golden mole of Africa has tiny eyes covered with a hairy skin and a tough, leathery pad on its nose. It finds its prey mostly by touch.

David Kirshner

energy until warmer weather comes. To hibernate, hedgehogs drop their body temperature close to that of the surrounding air. Their oxygen intake drops dramatically, and body functions slow down.

Moonrats

Moonrats are among the largest of the insectivores and can weigh up to 4½ pounds (2 kg). They look quite fierce with their rough, shaggy coats and the threatening way in which they open their mouths, showing a sharp set of pointy teeth.

▲ *Moonrats are not rodents but close relatives of hedgehogs. They get their name from their rat-like tail. They do not have spines but are covered in coarse hair. They mark their territory with scent. Scent glands near the tail give out a smell that we humans find most unpleasant.*

As sharp as they come!

The first thing you notice about a hedgehog is its thick coat of spines. An adult hedgehog has as many as 5,000 needle-sharp spines. Each one is ¾ to 1 inch (2 to 3 cm) long. The spines are special, strengthened hairs that are filled with pockets of air. They cover the back of the animal, while its belly is covered by rough skin and coarse hair.

When it is attacked, a hedgehog sticks its spines out in all directions — enough to frighten many enemies away! But if this does not work, the hedgehog rolls itself into a tight ball to protect the softer parts of its body.

▼ *The long-eared hedgehog lives in arid country. Its ears act as heat radiators.*

Eyal Bartov/Oxford Scientific Films

They live in wet areas, such as mangrove swamps, rubber plantations, and forests. Moonrats sleep during the day in hollow logs or under tree roots. At night they hunt for insects, frogs, fish, crustaceans, and mollusks — entering water to do so.

Shrews

Shrews are small, secretive animals. They have long, pointed noses, large ears, tiny eyes, and thick fur like velvet. The smallest of all the shrews weighs only $7/100$ ounce (2 g) and is the smallest mammal in the world. Shrews live in North and Central America, Europe, Asia, and most of Africa.

Shrews are very active animals — they are always on the go. These small mammals look for food in all kinds of places — in the water, on the land, and in the burrows of moles and other animals. They use their senses of hearing and smell to find prey and kill it right away. If they catch more food than they can eat, they store it in a safe place to eat later.

Shrews usually have 3 to 8 babies in a litter, depending on the species. The young take only 3 weeks to grow inside the mother's womb. They stay under-

A. & E. Bomford/Ardea London

▲ *Like most shrews, this common shrew is so small that it must feed continuously to maintain its body temperature. Without food, a shrew will die of starvation in as little as four hours.*

◄ *Young hedgehogs may look cute, but it is advisable not to get too close. Because of their spines, hedgehogs cannot groom themselves and become hosts to hundreds of parasites and fleas. They are also often infested with lice, ticks, and mites.*

David Kirshner

ground in a safe nest for another 3 weeks after they are born. Then the young shrews are encouraged to go on short foraging trips. During these trips, the young of some shrews have the strange habit of lining up and grabbing a tuft of hair on the rear end of the shrew in front. The one behind the mother holds on to her in the same way. This is called caravanning and helps the young to avoid danger.

Moles

Moles are specially adapted for living underground. They have broad, spade-like front legs and powerful shoulders

▲ *The Pyrenean desman lives in fast-flowing mountain streams. Its water-repellent coat traps air and makes the animal buoyant in water. If a desman on the stream bed lets go of the bottom or stops paddling, it pops to the surface like a cork.*

▶ *The bizarre-looking star-nosed mole of North America has a snout with twenty-two tentacles on it. Each tentacle has thousands of organs for sensing prey in the dark earth.*

Dwight R. Kuhn

30

for digging. A rather long head ends in a very sensitive pink snout. The sense of smell appears to be the most important sense for moles. Their tiny eyes and ears are covered by thick fur, but even so their hearing is acute. During the short breeding season males spend much time and energy locating mates. Mating takes place in the females' burrows. This is the only time that the two sexes are not aggressive toward each other.

Baby moles weigh less than $1/7$ ounce (4 g) when they are born. They are pink and hairless and depend on their mother for warmth. There are usually 3 babies in each mole litter. After about 5 weeks they go with their mother while she searches her burrow system for food. Soon they are ready to leave and build their own tunnels.

Desmans

There are two species of desman: the Pyrenean desman of northern Spain and Portugal and the Russian desman of Ukraine, Belarus, and western and central Russia. Just as the mole is built for living underground, so the desman is built for living in water. Its streamlined body glides along easily, propelled by strong, webbed hind limbs and steered by a long, broad tail.

Desmans eat the larvae of water-living insects such as the stone fly and caddis fly. They also eat small crustaceans such as shrimp, which they find by poking their long, flexible snouts under rocks and by clearing debris from the stream bed with long, sharp claws. They come up to the surface of the water to eat and to clean their fur before diving again.

Desmans build their nests on the banks of streams. The nests are made of leaves and dried grasses and are always built above water level. Desmans usually remain with one mate. In the spring, when mating takes place, the male protects his mate from other males and guards their food supply.

The young are looked after by the female and stay in the nest for about 7 weeks. They stay near their parents for about 2½ months, and then each goes off to find a mate and a territory of its own.

The mole patrol

Moles live in a tunnel system that also acts as a trap for earthworms and insect larvae. The mole patrols up and down its tunnels, ready to pounce on any food that happens to fall into them.

When the mole finds a worm, it bites off its head and pulls it through its front claws to squeeze grit and sand, which might damage the mole's teeth, from the worm's body. Severe tooth wear is a common cause of death in moles. If a large number of worms are caught, the mole stores them near its nest. It packs soil around the worms so that they stay alive but can't move until the mole is ready to eat them.

Building tunnels and looking after them take up a lot of the mole's time. When a mole starts to build, it begins with a straight tunnel about 22 yards (20 m) long and then adds side branches. This helps it find out where any neighboring animals are and forms a food trap for using later on. Other tunnels are built below the first ones so that the whole network runs along in layers, one on top of the other. Sometimes friendly moles will join their tunnels together.

Andy Purcell/Bruce Coleman Limited

▲ Moles are found over much of Europe, Asia, and North America. Their eyes are tiny and useless. Their huge, spade-like front legs are used for digging out tunnel systems, where they live and store food.

Tree Shrews

Tree shrews are little-known but fascinating mammals from the rain forests of eastern India and Southeast Asia. They are highly active, nervous, inquisitive, and generally aggressive animals. There are nineteen species of tree shrew alive today.

▲ *The large tree shrew has a long snout and strong digging claws.*

▼ *The common tree shrew lives in Malaysia and Sumatra. Although it lives in the trees, it often hunts for insects and lizards on the ground. The young are reared in a nest on their own. Their mother visits to feed them only every second day, so the babies suck until they are so full they cannot move.*

Rain forest mammals

One species, the feather-tailed or pen-tailed tree shrew, is different from all the rest. It lives on the Malay Peninsula and on the island of Borneo. This strange-looking animal is gray-brown in color and has large ears and long hairs on its face. It weighs less than 3 ounces (80 g) and is 12 to 14 inches (30 to 35 cm) long.

Its tail is covered with scales, except for the tip, which has long white hairs growing out at opposite sides. These hairs make its tail look like a feather. This strange tail helps the animal balance and feel things — while the shrew is awake, the tail twitches continuously.

Unlike other tree shrews, the feather-tailed variety hunts at night. Its favorite foods are fruit and insects, especially cockroaches, beetles, ants, and termites.

The other eighteen species live in eastern India and Southeast Asia. They can see better than their feather-tailed relatives and hunt during the day. Their brains are also better developed.

Tree shrews remain with one mate for life — which is usually 2 or 3 years. The male builds a nest of leaves a few days before the female gives birth. He then leaves and does not return until the young are about a month old. The babies are born with no hair and drink from their mother immediately after birth. Their main enemies are small meat-eating animals, snakes, and birds of prey such as hawks.

Flying Lemurs

Flying lemurs have a very misleading name: they can't fly, and they aren't lemurs! Rather, they glide through the trees of their rain forest home in Southeast Asia using their gliding membrane, or "skin wing."

Gerald Cubitt/Bruce Coleman Limited

▲ *Flying lemurs carry their young clinging to the mother's belly, or folded in a soft pouch made from her gliding membrane.*

Hanging around

Flying lemurs spend the day in the hollow of a tree or hanging upside-down under a branch. At night they glide from tree to tree in search of leaves, shoots, buds, flowers, and fruit.

These cat-size mammals have unusual incisors, rather like those of grass-eating mammals such as cattle or deer. Flying lemurs use their teeth for grooming and cleaning their fur and for rubbing and straining their food. Their feet are strongly clawed.

D. & W. Ward/Oxford Scientific Films

Natural hang-gliders

People sometimes wish they could glide through the air like a bird. Flying lemurs have a body that lets them do just that. They belong to a group of animals with a Latin name meaning "skin wing." This name describes the part of a flying lemur's body that is most unusual — the gliding membrane that stretches from the neck to the fingertips, along the sides of the body, between the toes, and joins the legs and tail. At full stretch the membrane spans more than 3 feet (1 m). The longest glide by a flying lemur ever recorded measured 435 feet (136 m).

◄ *Flying lemurs eat leaves, shoots, and buds of rain forest trees. Malayan flying lemurs like this one can be a nuisance on plantations, where they eat coconut flowers.*

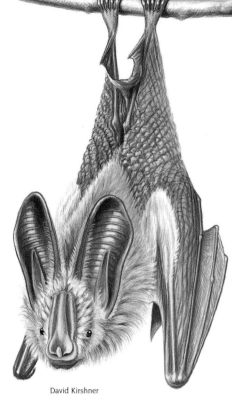

David Kirshner

▲ *The yellow-winged false vampire bat of Africa.*

▼ *In most insect-eating bats the tail helps to support a membrane between the hind limbs. Mouse-tailed bats have no such membrane and their tail dangles when they fly.*

Bats

Bats are the only mammals capable of true flight. Because most are active at night, they have developed a sophisticated sonar system to help them navigate and hunt. Bat species can be divided into two main groups: the Old World fruit bats and the generally smaller insect-eating bats.

Mammals that fly

Some 977 species of bat are currently recognized, making the order of bats second in number to that of the rodents. Most species are at home in the tropics and subtropics, but bats occur worldwide, except in the Antarctic, the colder area north of the Arctic Circle, and a few isolated islands.

The Greek name for the order is "Chiroptera," meaning "hand wing." Bats' wings are, in fact, modified hands. Their fingers are much longer than usual to support the flight membrane that stretches between them. The thumb is not usually joined to the membrane and it has a claw. Bats' feet are quite small but their toes have strong claws.

Bats' wings are pulled downward by muscles on the chest and upper arm. They are raised by other muscles on the back. Wing shapes vary. Usually, the bats that fly slowly through trees have short, wide wings, while bats that fly fast through open spaces have longer, narrower wings.

Bats' ears vary widely in size and shape. Some bats have exceptionally long ears. Many also have a tragus — a small projecting flap just inside the ear that obscures the ear opening. Several bat families have a noseleaf — a fleshy structure of skin around the nostrils.

Old World fruit bats

Fruit bats, flying foxes, and dog-faced fruit bats belong to the same family, in which there are more than 160 species. They are found in Asia, Australia, Africa, and many Pacific islands. They are medium to large bats with a simple ear whose edge forms a complete ring.

All fruit bats live on fruit, flowers, and nectar. Most are brown or black, some have speckled ears, and white spots or stripes on their faces. Most roost in trees or in the shadowy parts of caves.

Mouse-tailed bats

These small to medium-size bats are found from North Africa to southern Asia. They have large ears with a small tragus. They have no noseleaf, but the muzzle is swollen and ridged above slit-nostrils. As their name implies, they have a long thread-like tail. Mouse-tailed bats roost together in colonies.

Sheath-tailed bats

There are forty-nine species of bat in this family. Their tail is partly enclosed

Merlin D. Tuttle/Bat Conservation International

◄ *The tent-building bat roosts in a "tent" made by cutting through large leaves so that the edges curl inward.*

in the tail membrane so that only the tip sticks out. Most are brown, gray, or black, but one species, the ghost bat, is white. All these bats eat insects and roost in caves or trees.

Hog-nosed bat

The hog-nosed bat, or bumblebee bat, lives in caves in southwest Thailand. It has very large ears with a swollen tragus. It is the smallest known bat, with a head and body length of 1 to $1^{1}/_{3}$ inches (2.9 to 3.3 cm) — in fact, it ranks among the smallest of mammals and was discovered as recently as 1973.

Horseshoe bats

There are sixty-three species of horseshoe bat found in the tropics, subtropics, and temperate zones of the Old World (Europe, Asia, Australia, and Africa). They are small to medium in size with a horseshoe-shaped noseleaf. The few species that live in temperate zones hibernate in winter. They roost in caves, mines, hollow trees, or buildings.

New World leaf-nosed bats

There are 152 species in this family. Their muzzle has a simple, spear-shaped noseleaf. Most of them eat fruit and insects, some eat nectar and pollen, and some eat small invertebrates. The three species of vampire bat that belong to this family drink only blood. New World leaf-nosed bats have a wide variety of roosts, from caves to trees. Some species even build simple shelters.

Funnel-eared bats

Funnel-eared, or long-legged, bats live from Mexico to Brazil and in the Antilles islands. Their ears are very large and are funnel-shaped. The five species all eat insects and use caves, tunnels, or rock overhangs as roosts.

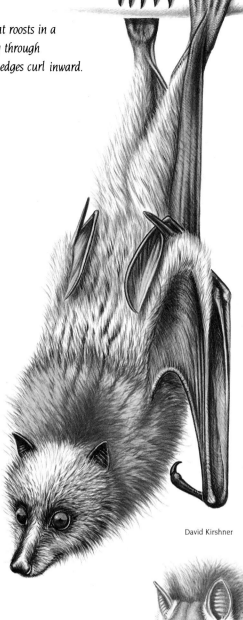

◄ *The gray-headed flying fox of Australia has large ears and excellent eyesight. It has a long snout and keen sense of smell, which it uses to find food and to detect other bats. It really does have a face like a fox's, doesn't it?*

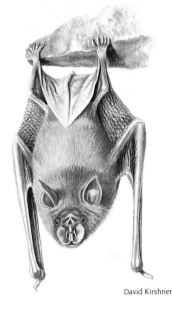

▲ *Orange individuals are not uncommon in otherwise drab-colored species of horseshoe bat. The horseshoe bat's tail is completely enclosed in the tail membrane. The horseshoe bat population in Europe is in sharp decline.*

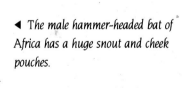

◄ *The male hammer-headed bat of Africa has a huge snout and cheek pouches.*

▲ *The sword-nosed bat, a New World leaf-nosed species, eats mainly insects.*

▲ *The Gambian epauletted fruit bat has tufts of hair on its shoulders that surround a scent gland.*

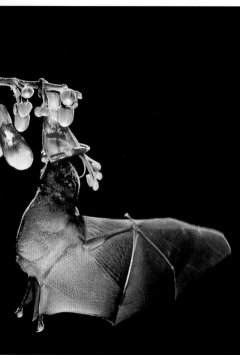

Merlin D. Tuttle/Bat Conservation International

▲ *The spear-nosed long-tongued bat can hover like a hummingbird while it sips nectar with its long tongue. In much the same way as a bee, it fertilizes the flowers of some trees in the American tropics.*

Disk-winged bats

The two species of disk-winged bats are found from southern Mexico to Peru and Brazil. These small mammals have a large, sticky disk on a short stalk at the base of each thumb and on the side of each foot from which they hang. They roost in family groups in rolled leaves or fronds in an unusual head-up position. When a roosting leaf unfurls, the bats move to a new one.

Vespertilionid bats

The name "vespertilionid" comes from the Latin word for "bat." There are 350 species in this family, which is the most widely distributed of bat families. Species in temperate zones hibernate or migrate in winter. They occupy all types of roosting site, including buildings. Most of them are brown, gray, or black, but some are more brightly colored or have white spots or stripes.

Free-tailed bats

There are about eighty-nine species of free-tailed bat. They have a wide muzzle, and the lips of many species are wrinkled. Their stout tail is wider than the tail membrane, and their legs are short and strong. One species, the hairless bat, has no hair on its body.

Free-tailed bats are very fast flyers. They form large colonies and roost together in caverns, tunnels, and hollow trees, or under leaves, rocks, bark, or in buildings.

Bat food

About 70 percent of bats feed on insects and other small arthropods such as spiders and scorpions. Bats capture insects in a number of ways: directly in the mouth; deflected into the mouth by the wing; or by scooping them up in the curled tail membrane. Bats play an important part in controlling insect populations.

A few species of bats also catch and eat frogs, lizards, small rodents, birds, and even other bats. Some catch fish, which they seize with their long claws and strong feet.

A smaller number feed on fruits, flowers, nectar, and pollen. These bats are confined to the tropics and

Vampires!

The three species of vampire bat are exceptional in that they live on the blood of other animals. They are found only in Central and South America, where populations of the common vampire bat have increased greatly since European colonization and the introduction of cattle and horses.

The bat's teeth are so sharp that it need only lay them very gently on an animal's skin to cause a small cut. The victim is usually unaware it is being "bitten." Blood is lapped from the wound. Some vampire bats in Central and South America are known to carry rabies. The vast majority of bats do not normally bite humans, and only a few human deaths caused by bat bites have been recorded. It is advisable never to handle a sick or dead bat, especially in North and South America.

Merlin D. Tuttle/Bat Conservation International

▲ *The vampire bat feeds only on blood. Its razor-sharp teeth make a small cut in the victim's flesh — in this case a fowl — and blood is lapped from the wound.*

Stephen Dalton/NHPA

Flying in the dark

Bats are nocturnal creatures — and while Old World fruit bats have large eyes and can see well enough in the dark to move around and find food, insect-eating bats navigate by means of ultrasound, or echolocation.

Ultrasonic sounds have a very high frequency and cannot be detected by the human ear. Bats produce these sounds in their throats and emit them through their mouths or nostrils. Bats with noseleaves use them to focus and direct the sound.

As it sends out these high-pitched squeaks the bat closes its ears so it will not deafen itself. The ultrasound waves bounce off surrounding objects — the ground, trees, buildings, and also other moving objects in the air, such as insects. The bat's ears pick up

the returning echo, and its brain calculates its relationship to fixed and moving objects around it.

A hunting bat in flight will search for prey by emitting 5 to 10 pulses per second. Once a flying insect has been detected, the bat increases the pulses to as many as 200 per second, to give it continuous information on its victim.

The strength of the reflected vibrations tells the bat its distance from its prey. The slight differences in the time taken for the vibrations to reach each ear tell the bat in which direction its prey lies. This sonar system is so sensitive and accurate that bats are able to fly swiftly between telephone wires without touching them.

▲ *To be able to chase and capture a moth in the blackest of nights, like this horseshoe bat, seems an astonishing feat. Even more remarkable is the fact that the bat recognizes all other objects in its vicinity — the ground, trees, bushes, rocks, other bats, and owls. It "sees" by means of ultrasound.*

subtropics, where food is available throughout the year. They perform the vital tasks of spreading seeds and pollinating flowers.

Birth control

Both male and female bats can store sperm in their reproductive tracts during winter or hibernation. Fertilization usually occurs the following spring. Some tropical bats are also able to slow

the development of the baby bat inside the mother's womb.

This ensures that the young bats are born at those times of the year when the most food is available. The smaller species of bat have a gestation period of 40 to 60 days before they are born. The larger species have a gestation period of up to 8 months. Usually only 1 bat is born at a time, but some species quite often have twins, while others can have up to 5 babies.

Lemurs and Tarsiers

Lemurs and tarsiers belong to an order of mammals known as primates. The word "primate" comes from Latin and means "chief" or "head." The order of primates also includes monkeys, apes, and humans.

Lemurs

There are five families of lemur. Four of these families are confined to the island of Madagascar. Two species on the island were discovered as late as 1987 and 1988, when they were on the brink of extinction. The fifth family comprises lorises and bushbabies, found in Africa, Sri Lanka, southern India, and Southeast Asia.

Dwarf and mouse lemurs Dwarf and mouse lemurs live alone on their own territory. The tiny mouse lemurs are the smallest of all the primates, weighing a mere 1¾ to 2 ounces (50 to 60 g). They eat mainly insects. The larger dwarf lemurs eat fruit as well as insects.

"True" lemurs The ring-tailed lemur is about 3 feet (1 m) in length — more than half of which is tail. These lemurs live mainly on the ground in open forests, in troops of 12 to 20 animals. Females are dominant and win disputes with males over favorite foods or territory.

Male lemurs have wrist glands with horny spurs. They rub the spurs onto small trees with a little click, leaving a slash in the bark filled with their scent. This scent tells other lemurs which male has been there and which troop holds the territory.

Ring-tailed lemurs, like all lemurs, are seasonal breeders. All mating occurs during April, and the gestation period is 136 days. Lemurs give birth to a single young. It rides around with its mother, clinging to her fur, until it gradually becomes independent.

Indris The black-and-white indri is the largest surviving lemur and the only one that has almost no tail. It has long hind legs and moves by jumping from tree to tree.

Indris are active by day and sleep at night. Their loud, wailing cries float through the forest, warning neighbors of territorial boundaries.

The two other species of indri are smaller and have long tails.

▼ A ring-tailed lemur mother seeks shelter from the midday sun for herself and her baby — can you spot its tail? — in the middle canopy of the rain forest.

Walt Anderson/Tom Stack & Associates

David Kirshner

◄ *The nocturnal gray mouse lemur (far left) is the smallest of all the primates. The aye-aye (top center) is rare and secretive. The Philippine tarsier (top right) has enormous eyes, and in one species the skull has become wider than it is long to accommodate them. The angwantibo, or golden potto (bottom), is a small loris found in West Central Africa.*

Aye-aye The secretive aye-aye is black with rough shaggy fur, a very long tail, and huge ears and eyes. It is solitary and nocturnal. This unusual mammal has a single pair of huge incisors in each jaw that grow continuously. These teeth are used for gnawing away the bark of trees to get at grubs. The aye-aye has extremely long fingers and toes. The middle finger of each hand is especially long and as thin as wire for reaching into tree crevices to find grubs.

Lorises and bushbabies These lemur-like creatures differ little from the Malagasy lemurs. The lorises of south and Southeast Asia, and the potto and angwantibo of Africa, have short limbs and a short tail. They move in a rather slow, gliding way, using their strong hands and feet to grip round branches.

The bushbabies, or galagos, of Africa have long, bushy tails and long back legs, and move by jumping.

Bushbabies are so called because of their human-like cries.

Tarsiers

Tarsiers look more like rat-tailed bushbabies than monkeys. They have long back legs, long skinny fingers and toes, huge eyes, and big ears. They live on the islands of Southeast Asia.

Tarsiers live in pairs in forest areas. They are active at night and feed on insects, lizards, and other small vertebrates. Tarsiers are not uncommon but are seldom seen, which is probably why their Indonesian name means "ghost animal."

▲ *The indri (top), a very rare lemur, is larger than its relatives and has only a stump of a tail. It is now protected in the mountain rain forest reserve of Perinet in northeastern Madagascar. The red-ruffed lemur (bottom) is just as rare and has just as restricted a range.*

39

New World Monkeys

New World monkeys live in the rain forests of South and Central America. They have nostrils that point sideways, and their thumbs are not obviously opposable to their other fingers. The larger species have prehensile tails — no other primate has a prehensile tail.

Scientists are puzzled as to how these monkeys got to America. Their closest living relatives are African monkeys. The earliest remains of American monkeys are 35 million years old — the continents of South America and Africa broke up long before this.

David Kirshner

Marmosets and tamarins Marmosets and tamarins are the only monkeys to have claws. They range in size from the world's smallest living monkey, the pygmy marmoset weighing 4½ ounces (125 g), to the golden lion tamarin weighing 21 ounces (600 g). All but one species of marmoset give birth to twins. The young stay with their parents after they have matured to help rear the next pair of babies, and the next.

Night monkeys and titis Pairs of titis seem to form close relationships and will sit side by side with their tails intertwined. Night monkeys do not seem as closely bonded.

David Kirshner

▲ The cotton-top tamarin is a rare species of primate that lives in Panama.

▶ The strange-looking red uakari is the only New World monkey without a long tail.

David Kirshner

▲ The night monkey is the only monkey that is active by night. It is widespread in South America.

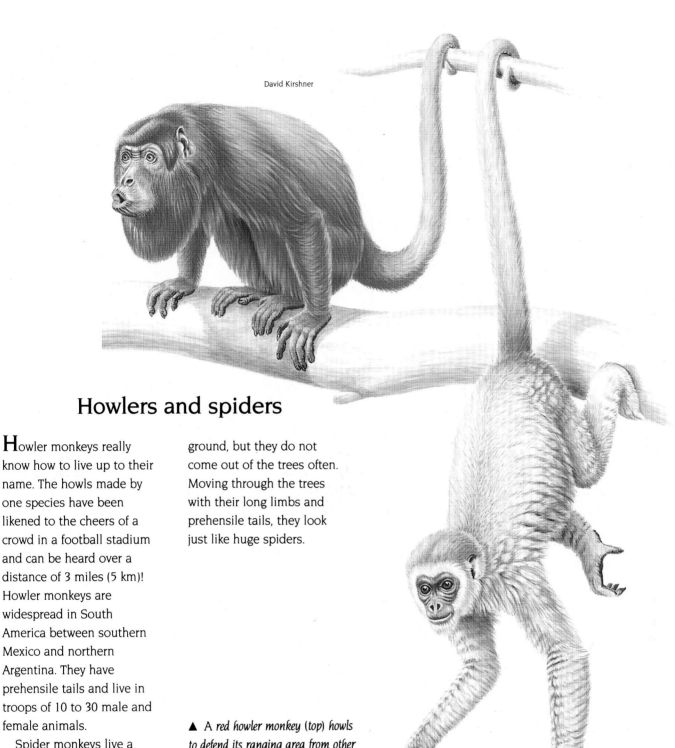

David Kirshner

Howlers and spiders

Howler monkeys really know how to live up to their name. The howls made by one species have been likened to the cheers of a crowd in a football stadium and can be heard over a distance of 3 miles (5 km)! Howler monkeys are widespread in South America between southern Mexico and northern Argentina. They have prehensile tails and live in troops of 10 to 30 male and female animals.

Spider monkeys live a more active life than howlers. Their troops are much larger, and small groups go out each day looking for food.

Spider monkeys are able to run on two legs on the ground, but they do not come out of the trees often. Moving through the trees with their long limbs and prehensile tails, they look just like huge spiders.

▲ *A red howler monkey (top) howls to defend its ranging area from other troops. Red howlers are the biggest of their family. The woolly spider monkey, or muriqui (bottom), is the largest and rarest of all the New World monkeys — only about 300 survive in the dry forests of southeastern Brazil.*

Squirrel monkeys Squirrel monkeys are small, greenish monkeys with white faces and black muzzles. The females weigh 18 to 26 ounces (500 to 750 g) and the males weigh about 2 pounds (1 kg) more. They live in large troops of 20 to 50 animals, with more females than males. Their breeding season lasts for 3 to 4 months. At this time the males put on weight and become very aggressive as they compete for mating opportunities.

N. Tanaka, Orion Press/Bruce Coleman Limited

▲ The Japanese macaque, or snow monkey, lives in Honshu Island's northern mountains, which are snow-covered for more than half the year. During the winter they survive by eating bark.

Old World Monkeys

There are two major groups of Old World monkeys — the ones that eat leaves and have stomachs like kangaroos or cows, and the ones that have simple stomachs and pouches in the lining of their cheeks for storing food. Old World monkeys live in Asia and Africa.

Guenons

Guenons are a marvelously varied and brightly colored lot. In rain forests the three species of guenons live happily together high in the trees. Each small troop consists of one male, three or four females, and their young. Although the troops have their own territory, each one may consist of monkeys from two, or even three, of these species.

Baboons and their relatives

The gelada is a large baboon-like monkey of the grasslands of Ethiopia, in Africa. The male of the species is much larger than the female and has an enormous mane. Geladas live in a troop of one male and one or several females. Gelada troops form huge herds of perhaps several hundred animals, which forage for food on clifftops.

The hamadryas baboon, like the gelada, lives in a one-male group. Savanna baboons, on the other hand, live in troops ranging from about ten to several hundred animals — there are many adult males as well as females in these troops. Hamadryas and savanna baboons have interbred in northern Ethiopia, where their ranges meet.

Other relatives of the baboon include the drill and mandrill, the mangabeys, the talapoin, and the swamp monkey.

Macaques

Macaques live in Asia and, like the savanna baboons of Africa, belong to troops with many males in them. Some species live mainly on the ground, while others prefer trees.

The crab-eating, or long-tailed, macaque lives in Southeast Asia and is one of the smaller species. It is closely related to the rhesus monkey, which lives in forest areas of northern India and China.

Colobid monkeys

Most species of colobid monkeys live in Asia, while only seven species live in Africa. Their specialized digestive systems — adapted to eat leaves — are unique among primates and are similar to the digestive systems of ruminants and kangaroos.

Colobus monkeys gallop, rather than walk, along branches and, at the end of the branch, launch themselves into space without breaking stride and land in the neighboring tree, grabbing hold with their hook-like, thumbless hands.

The Asian colobids differ from their African relatives by having short thumbs. The sacred langur of India and Sri Lanka represents the monkey-god Hanuman of Hindu mythology. It is often fed when it wanders near towns.

The largest colobid of all is the brick-red proboscis monkey of Borneo, which seems as much at home in water as it does in trees. Young proboscis monkeys have long, forward-pointing noses. In females these stop growing at maturity, but in males the snouts keep growing into enormous, drooping lobes.

Francisco Futil/Bruce Coleman Limited

▲ The hamadryas baboon lives in rocky and arid areas in northern Ethiopia and southwestern Arabia.

▼ The diana monkey, or diana guenon, lives in the rapidly disappearing high forests of West Africa.

▼ The male mandrill of Central Africa is more brightly colored than the female and young of the species.

David Kirshner

David Kirshner

▶ Only the adult male gelada has a long mane. Both male and female geladas have a bright red patch of bare skin on their chests

David Kirshner

Gibbons

Gibbons are the smallest of the ape family. They are only distant relatives of the great apes and humans. They are slender mammals with extraordinarily long arms, long legs, and long, narrow hands.

▼ *These white-handed gibbons are still quite common in the forests of the Malay Peninsula. But they will only survive as long as their forest habitat remains intact.*

Swinging through the trees

Gibbons move rapidly through the trees using a hand-over-hand technique and sometimes drop to a lower branch or jump to another tree.

A male and female gibbon with up to four offspring occupy a treetop territory. The largest gibbon of all is the siamang, which weighs 20 to 27½ pounds (9 to 12.5 kg). Both sexes are black and have very large throat sacs, which are inflated before calling. Their calls are quite deafening.

Siamangs eat a lot of leaves and some fruit. They have fairly small territories and live in closely bonded pairs. The adult male carries and babysits the young gibbon until it is at least a year old.

The best known species of gibbon is the white-handed gibbon. These small gibbons weigh about 11 to 15 pounds (5 to 7 kg). They are remarkable for their very dense fur: they have more than 11,000 hairs per square inch (1,700 hairs per square cm) of skin. This is two or three times more fur than most monkeys.

Jean-Paul Ferrero/Auscape International

44

▲ Muller's gibbon lives in Borneo. It is a close relative of the white-handed gibbon.

45

The Canid Family

The family of mammals called Canids can be divided into four groups: foxes; dogs and wolves; the South American canids; and the raccoon dog and bat-eared fox.

Fast runners

Canids live in open grasslands and are adapted for fast running after prey. They originated in North America about 57 to 37 million years ago and are now found throughout the world. The dogs that so many families keep as pets are thought to have evolved from a wolf-like ancestor.

Canids rely on hearing and smell to find food. Their teeth and digestive systems have adapted to allow them to eat all kinds of things, including small vertebrates such as rabbits and mice, insects, fruit, mollusks such as snails, and carrion (the flesh of dead animals).

Canids have a long face and usually two molars (grinding teeth) in each jaw. They live on the ground and have long bushy tails, long legs, and slim bodies. Only one species, the North American gray fox, can climb trees easily. All canids have large, pointed ears and a uniquely formed internal ear — different from that of cats.

Foxes

Foxes are small canids with very pointed skulls and bushy tails. All foxes eat the same sort of food — any small animals, as well as insects and fruit.

The desert foxes are the smallest species. They are pale to blend with their sandy surroundings and have enormous ears to help them radiate heat and locate prey. The fennec fox is one example and weighs 1 to 3 pounds

▼ The red wolf of North America is in danger of extinction. Its range is gradually being taken over by people, and large numbers have been shot by hunters and farmers. It now survives only in captivity.

David Kirshner

▲ The maned wolf of South America has long, stilt-like legs adapted for the long prairie grass in which it lives. It is a predator of such mammals as rabbits, pacas, and armadillos.

▶ The African hunting dog, unlike other canids, eats only meat. It hunts for prey such as zebra or antelope, in packs of 6 to 12 dogs. These dogs are good parents and have large litters of up to 16 pups.

46

(500 g to 1.5 kg). The Arctic fox is larger and has either a brown or a steel-gray summer coat. Both color types change to a pure white winter coat for camouflage in the snow.

The more widespread red fox has settled in all areas of northern and central Europe, Asia, and northern America. It is adaptable to all habitats — from mountainous regions to lowland forests to town suburbs. The red fox continues to spread and is pushing into the Arctic region, where it threatens to compete with the Arctic fox for food.

Dogs and wolves

Within this group are the most social of the canid species. Wolf packs, for instance, have a well-developed social structure and are led by a dominant breeding pair. Wolves, as well as Indian dholes and African hunting dogs, hunt in packs. Six to twelve animals together are able to capture much bigger prey.

▼ *The bat-eared fox of Africa eats mostly insects. Four to eight extra molars provide it with more chewing surfaces for these insects. Its very large ears help it find food and radiate extra body heat.*

David Kirshner

Hans Reinhard/Bruce Coleman Limited

▼ *The gray fox of North America is the only canid that can climb trees easily. It is often tamed and kept as a pet.*

▲ *These are cubs of the red, or common, fox. Foxes are not afraid to venture into towns and gardens and often raid trash cans at night.*

David Kirshner

◀ *The raccoon dog of Asia is the only canid that does not bark. Unlike other members of its family, it lives in the dense undergrowth of forests. Its thick coat is prized by the fur* industry.

David Kirshner

47

Raccoons and Coatis

The inquisitive raccoon is familiar to most people in North America. These small mammals are mainly omnivores, eating both animals and plants. Coatis are close relatives of raccoons.

Raccoons

The favorite food of raccoons lives in the water and includes frogs, fish, and crustaceans such as crabs. Raccoons have the habit of washing food with their front paws before eating.

They are nocturnal, solitary, and live in forest areas, where they find dens in hollow trees and rock crevices. The raccoon sleeps in winter but does not hibernate. Because it cannot reduce its body functions, it uses up half its body weight to stay warm and emerges in spring looking very gaunt.

Coatis

Coatis also live in forests and woodlands, but they are diurnal (active by day rather than by night). Coatis vary dramatically in color, with gray, red, and brown young often born in one litter.

Coatis are omnivores like raccoons, but they eat insects and roots rather than fish. Females and young live in bands of 4 to 50 animals. They spread out and comb the forest floor, digging up roots and poking their long snouts into crevices looking for food. Their tails help them balance when they are up in the trees.

Adult males are allowed into the group only during the mating period. After one dominant male has mated with the females, the young males are expelled from the group.

▼ *The ringtail is the smallest member of the raccoon family but is also one of the most carnivorous. It eats lizards and small mammals as well as fruit and nuts.*

David Kirshner

▼ *This ringtail coati of South America is about to poke its flexible snout into the log to expose the insects that form much of its diet.*

David Kirshner

David Kirshner

▲ *The kinkajou lives in tropical American forests, feeding mainly upon fruits and nectar. It is one of very few carnivores to have a prehensile tail. Although a member of the raccoon family, the kinkajou lacks the distinctive black face mask and tail rings.*

Konrad Wothe/Bruce Coleman Limited

The Mustelid Family

▲ *The wolverine, or glutton, has a thick winter coat that is prized by Eskimos.*

W̲ith nearly double the number of species of any other carnivore family, the Mustelids — weasels, otters, skunks, and badgers — are clearly the most successful. They are found in nearly every type of habitat, including salt and fresh water, and on every continent except Australia and Antarctica.

▼ *The South American tayra is a member of the weasel family that lives in trees rather than on the ground. It feeds mainly on fruit.*

Weasels, martens, and wolverines

Weasels have short round ears, very long bodies, and short tails. They feed at night and mostly underground, where they chase mice, rats, and other rodents into their burrows.

Martens are large arboreal weasels. The largest marten, the fisher, feeds heavily on spined, tree-living porcupines. The marten skillfully attacks the porcupine's head, where there are no quills, and when it is dead, flips it over and feeds from its underside.

The wolverine is the largest member of this family. It is about 1,000 times heavier than the smallest species, the "least weasel." The wolverine body is strong and its legs are short. It lives in the colder parts of Europe, Asia, and North America and is very good at killing fairly large animals in deep snow.

Erwin & Peggy Bauer/Bruce Coleman Limited

49

▲ *This striped skunk is enjoying a refreshing swim in the river. Skunks don't take to the water often, but they can, like most mammals, swim when necessary.*

▼ *Sea otters spend almost all their time in water. This one is cradling a pup.*

Badgers

Badgers have thick strong bodies, short legs, and powerful jaws. The North American badger lives alone and feeds on small rodents such as rabbits. It uses its powerful front legs and claws to burrow after prey.

The Eurasian badger is a bit bigger than the North American variety. It lives in social groups of up to 12 animals that defend a territory. It eats mainly earthworms and grubs. Badger pairs usually bond for life. Living burrows are continuously expanded and may be used by generations of badger.

Otters

Otters spend most of their time in water. They have webbed feet and stiff whiskers and are at home in both salt and fresh water. Their strong tails propel them through the water.

Most freshwater otters live alone, but sea otters are more sociable. They form separate groups of males and females at different coastal areas. Sea otters often use "tools," such as flat rocks, to break open mollusk shells.

Skunks

Skunks are infamous for the foul-smelling liquid that they propel from an anal gland when threatened. Their vivid black-and-white coloring warns enemies not to come too close. Skunks are omnivores and like to feed on small animals such as mice, as well as insects.

Small Cat-like Carnivores

Frans Lanting/Minden Pictures

▲ *The ring-tailed mongoose of Madagascar hunts in trees for small reptiles, mammals, and birds.*

M ost cat-like carnivores — including the cat family itself — live on land. The group includes civets and genets, mongooses, and of course cats.

Civets and genets

Civets and genets are the least studied of the carnivores. This is possibly because they are difficult to observe. Various species live in southern Europe, Africa, and southern Asia.

Civets and genets are nocturnal, solitary hunters. Some species are quite common, like the common palm civet that raids coffee plantations. It is sometimes called the toddy cat because it loves fermented palm sap (toddy).

Mongooses

These small meat-eaters have long, slender bodies, well adapted for chasing animals down burrows, though they mostly eat insects. They are found from deserts to tropical rain forests in Africa, the Middle East, India, and Southeast Asia. Because they prey on rats they were introduced to many islands, where they in turn are now considered pests.

Hyenas

The hyena is one of the most fearsome of predators on the open plains of Africa. It looks very like a wolf or dog, but has long forelimbs, short hind limbs, and a mane on its back. The hyena has a large head and a massive jaw muscle that gives it one of the strongest bites of all carnivores. Its strong teeth are adapted for crushing bones, making the hyena a good scavenger. It often eats the remains of animals that have been killed by other animals. The females of the spotted hyena are bigger than the males and give birth to 1 to 4 young.

Small cats

Twenty-nine of the thirty-seven species of wild cat are classed as small cats. Many species are endangered and do not seem to breed well in captivity.

David Kirshner

◀ *The caracal of Africa and west Asia is about the size of a springer spaniel. It hunts mainly at night and can take quite large prey, such as impala.*

▼ *The jaguarundi of North and South America is about the size of a large domestic cat. It hunts mainly during the day and eats small mammals, insects, birds, and fruit.*

David Kirshner

David Kirshner

◀ *The African civet is the largest of its family.*

▲ *Baird's tapir of Central America is a swamp-dweller. It forages for leaves and shoots with its long, flexible, trunk-like snout.*

Tapirs

Tapirs are rare, strange creatures. They are distantly related to equids (horses and asses) and to the rhinoceros. The life of the tapir has changed little in 20 million years.

Camouflaged browsers

The tapir is a squat animal that weighs about 660 pounds (300 kg). It has a short trunk at the tip of its snout. There are three South American species and one Asian species.

While the American species are a dull brown or gray, the Malayan tapir is a contrasting black and white. All young tapirs are patterned with pale stripes and flecks on a dark background. This camouflages them, making them hard to spot in the dappled light of the forest.

Tapirs eat forest shrubs and herbs, as well as fruit and seeds. By feeding on large fruits, they probably play an important role in scattering the seeds of many forest trees.

Tapirs spend a great deal of time in water, but because they are nocturnal, it is hard to tell just how much time. They are also fond of wallowing in mud.

The survival of tapirs is threatened by logging and forest clearing in both Asia and South America.

Hyraxes

This solidly built little mammal is often mistaken for a rabbit or rodent. But the hyrax is so different from all other mammals that zoologists place it in an order of its own.

Hyraxes live in the dry, rocky areas of Africa and the Arabian Peninsula. Living in a habitat with sparse food, hyraxes have adapted to a low-energy diet. When they leave their sleeping holes in the morning, they huddle together for warmth and bask in the sun.

These mammals walk on the soles of their very unusual feet. The feet have large, rubbery-soft pads that are kept moist by special glands and give the hyrax a firm grip on rocks and trees.

Hyraxes can live to be 10 years old. They are sociable and live in colonies of up to 80 animals. All species eat plants and sometimes invertebrates. Both rock and tree hyraxes find food on the ground. While the colony forages, a few individuals keep watch for predators. Hyraxes are hunted by leopards, wild dogs, eagles, pythons, and humans.

▼ *Forty to fifty million years ago, hyraxes of all sizes were the dominant grazing mammals of North Africa. They have since been replaced by antelopes, cattle, sheep, and goats. Surviving species of hyrax, like this southern tree hyrax, are the size of a rabbit.*

▼ *Yellow-spotted rock hyraxes bask in the sun on an old termite mound. Although they look like guinea-pigs, hyraxes are most closely related to elephants, sea cows, and aardvarks.*

Peter Davey/Bruce Coleman Limited

John Shaw/NHPA

Blood-curdling screams

No other animal sounds like a hyrax. The young have only five of the twenty-one sounds made by adults, but their vocabulary changes and increases throughout life.

Tree hyraxes begin to call soon after dark with a series of croaks that ends in a loud scream. These screams are so blood-curdling that travelers on safari in Africa often mistake them for attacking bandits.

Aardvarks

The African aardvark is one of the strangest of all living mammals. It eats ants but is not an anteater; it has ears like a donkey's; and it looks like a long-nosed pig. In many ways, it can be thought of as a living fossil.

Thick-skinned mammals

The name "aardvark" comes from Dutch and means "earth pig." Aardvarks are pig-like animals with thick skin that protects them from the bites of the ants and termites on which they feed.

Their front legs are short, powerful digging tools. Aardvarks can excavate a termite mound in just a few minutes. As well as ants and termites, aardvarks eat the fruits of a wild South African plant known as aardvark cucumber. They also like locusts, grasshoppers, and beetles.

When attacked, aardvarks are fierce and will slash and kick with their legs and claws. They can also do a speedy somersault and stand on their back legs and tails to defend themselves with their front feet.

Usually, aardvarks are found anywhere that termites live. When looking for food, aardvarks move in a zigzag path, sniffing the ground in a strip 33 yards (30 m) wide. They may travel as much as 18 miles (30 km) in one night.

Aardvarks dig three types of burrows: for food, for temporary shelter, and for living in. Abandoned burrows are important for the survival of many smaller animals, such as hyraxes, which use them as dens or as refuges.

The presence of aardvarks in farming areas helps control the pests that destroy crops. But their burrows can be hazardous to vehicles and galloping horses. Aardvarks are hunted for their meat and hide.

◄ It's unusual to see an aardvark running about during the day. They usually sleep all day in their burrows and emerge only at night.

Pigs and Peccaries

Pigs originated in Africa, where giant species appeared early in the Ice Ages. The pigs of the Old World and the peccaries of the New World are not related but have evolved in similar ways.

There are eight species of pig and three species of peccary. Both mammals eat roots and tubers that grow underground. Pigs also eat carrion, birds' nests, newborn mammals, and small rodents.

Peccaries

Peccaries live in closely knit groups of up to a hundred animals that jointly defend territories. Both males and females are fighters; they have sharp teeth and are alike in appearance.

Pigs

Female wild boars shelter their many tiny young from the cold, snow, and rain by building domed nests and sitting in the nests to provide extra warmth. Female pigs live in mother-daughter groups on large home ranges.

Pigs are not known to defend territories and they share resources, making them ideal for domestication. Escaped domestic pigs in North America, Australia, and New Zealand have reestablished feral populations.

▼ *The chacoan peccary was first discovered in 1975. It is the largest and rarest of the three species of peccary found in the Americas. Its massive head indicates that it is descended from large ancestors.*

David Kirshner

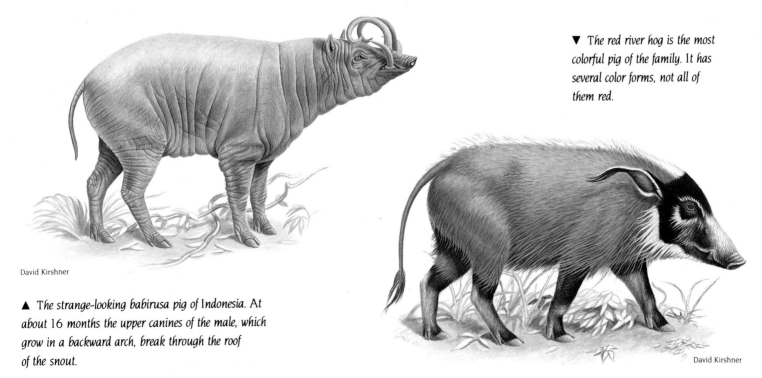

David Kirshner

▲ *The strange-looking babirusa pig of Indonesia. At about 16 months the upper canines of the male, which grow in a backward arch, break through the roof of the snout.*

▼ *The red river hog is the most colorful pig of the family. It has several color forms, not all of them red.*

David Kirshner

Cloven-hoofed Mammals

David Kirshner

▲ The saiga is an antelope from the colder parts of eastern Asia. Its downward-pointing nostrils and rather odd snout are thought to filter dust from, and warm, the air before it reaches the lungs.

There are very few small members of this group of mammals. Most — such as giraffes and camels — are very big. But the species described and illustrated on this page and the next two pages are the exceptions to the rule.

Small bovids

All mammals in the bovid family — cattle, oxen, sheep, goats, antelopes, and many other species — graze on grasses and other plants, chew the cud, and have curved horns on their heads.

Bovids originated in Africa, Asia, and Europe. Nowadays they can be found all over the world in all sorts of climates. There are no native bovids in South America or Australia, but many have been introduced in the last few hundred years.

David Kirshner

▲ The mountain anoa, or dwarf water buffalo, is the smallest of the true cattle. It is also the oldest surviving representative of wild cattle. The anoa lives only on the island of Celebes (now Sulawesi). It is excitable and dangerous if cornered.

David Kirshner

▲ The bighorn sheep of North America lives in a wide variety of habitats — from cold alpine areas to hot deserts.

▶ The four-horned antelope of India is the only member of this group to have four horns. It shows features of both cattle and antelopes.

56

David Kirshner

David Kirshner

▲ The klipspringer is a dwarf antelope that lives in rocky country in many parts of Africa south of the Sahara Desert. It jumps on the tips of its hooves with great agility.

▼ The Himalayan tahr is a wild, long-haired goat. Only adult males have the magnificent mane. This species has been successfully introduced to New Zealand.

David Kirshner

David Kirshner

▼ The wild goat of Western Asia is the ancestor of all the domestic breeds we know today. Male goats and sheep need large horns like these because they compete with each other by butting their heads together.

◄ Duikers are small, short-horned antelopes that browse at the forest edge. "Duiker" is an Afrikaans word for "diver." They were given this name because of their habit of diving into the undergrowth and lying low when frightened.

◄ The Barbary sheep, or aoudad, of northern Africa is an endangered species.

David Kirshner

David Kirshner

David Kirshner

▶ The Indian muntjac is a small Asian deer that has very simple antlers and sharp, pointed canine teeth, or tusks.

Pudu

The pudu is the smallest species of deer. It is only 14 to 15 inches (35 to 38 cm) high at the shoulder. There are two species: the northern pudu of Peru, Ecuador, and Columbia, and the southern pudu of the rain forests of Chile and Argentina.

Muntjac

This small member of the deer family lives in Asia and weighs about 48 pounds (22 kg). The muntjac eats leaves, bark, fruit, and carrion.

Muntjacs are either solitary or move about in pairs or in small family groups.

Water chevrotain

The water chevrotain of West African rain forests is about the size of a rabbit and has large canine teeth that never stop growing. Water chevrotains bark loudly to signal danger.

Although they look rather like small deer, water chevrotains are very different in many respects. They belong to a group called the tragulids, which are the most primitive of the cloven-hoofed mammals.

▶ The tiny pudu, the smallest species of deer, has simple, unbranched antlers.

David Kirshner

David Kirshner

▶ The water chevrotain protects itself with its sharp canine teeth. These teeth never stop growing.

Pangolins

This extraordinary-looking animal looks more like a reptile than a mammal. It is the only mammal to have a covering of horny scales.

Mammals with scales

The seven species of pangolin, or scaly anteater, live in Southeast Asia and in the tropical and subtropical parts of Africa. The male pangolin is much bigger than the female. All pangolins have short, powerful limbs, which they use for digging into termite mounds and anthills. Most pangolins are active at night. The ground-living species also use their claws for scooping out underground burrows, where they live during the day. The tree-living species find tree hollows to curl up in during daylight hours. Pangolins have bad eyesight and average hearing but a very good sense of smell.

Pangolins feed exclusively on insects, mainly termites and ants, which they catch with their long tongues. A pangolin's tongue is 27 inches (70 cm) long. It remains folded back into a pouch in the animal's throat when not being used. As pangolins have no teeth, all food is crushed in a part of the stomach. The stomach usually contains small pebbles to assist in grinding food. When pangolins are feeding, a thick membrane protects their eyes and special muscles block off their nostrils to keep ants out.

In Africa, large numbers of pangolins are killed every year for their meat. In China, pangolin scales are used in traditional medicines.

But the greatest threat to the survival of these mammals is the destruction of tropical rain forests.

▼ *The pangolin's scales protect every part of its body except the underside and the inner parts of the limbs. The scales are made of horn and grow from the thick underlying skin.*

Armed and dangerous

Not only is the pangolin armored with scales, but it carries a lethal weapon — its tail. Even though it is covered in scales, the tail can be moved about fairly easily. In some species it is prehensile.

The tail of all pangolin species has a sensitive end that can be used as a hook. When an enemy threatens, the pangolin lashes out its amazing tail and cuts and slashes with the razor-sharp scales. At the same time, the animal may spray its attacker with a revolting-smelling fluid from the anal gland.

C.B. Frith/Bruce Coleman Limited

David Kirshner

▲ *Ground squirrels are social animals and live in family groups in burrows. They are constantly on the alert for danger and issue alarm calls to the others if they spot an enemy.*

Rodents

R odents are the world's most successful mammals and are found in just about every habitat on earth. There are three main groups: squirrel-like rodents, mouse-like rodents, and cavy-like rodents.

Squirrel-like rodents

The group we call squirrel-like rodents lives in all parts of the world except for Australia, Polynesia, southern South America, and the Sahara and Arabian deserts.

Beavers The mountain beaver lives in the pine forests of North America, where it builds an elaborate burrow. The North American beaver and the European beaver are larger herbivores (plant-eaters). They spend half their life in the water and have streamlined bodies, a flattened tail, and webbed feet.

Beavers live in family groups consisting of an adult pair and the offspring of several years (they have one litter each year). They cut down trees with their teeth and use them for food and for building dams across streams. The dams cause ponds to form. When this happens, the beavers build a lodge shaped like a cone in the pond, with the entrance to the living chamber through an underwater tunnel.

Squirrels Squirrels live on all continents except Australia. Tree squirrels are active little animals. They have excellent eyesight and move easily through the trees with the help of sharp claws and a bushy tail that acts as a counterbalance. On the ground they move with a series of arched leaps. They

▶ *The African spring hare is a very large burrowing rodent. It is not a hare but a relative of the scaly-tailed squirrel. It has an upright posture and is an excellent jumper, covering 24 feet (8 m) in one bound if necessary.*

G. Cubitt/Bruce Coleman Limited

eat fruit, nuts, seeds, shoots, leaves, and sometimes insects.

Flying squirrels glide rather than fly, using a membrane down each side of the body as a parachute and the tail as a rudder. When they land, flying squirrels brake by stretching the body and tail upward.

Ground squirrels are widespread and include prairie dogs in America, marmots across the Northern Hemisphere, and chipmunks. Many of them live in burrows, where they raise young, store food, and hide from enemies.

Pocket gophers and pocket mice Both these families have external, fur-lined "pockets" or pouches in their cheeks for holding and carrying food. Pocket gophers, found in North and Central America, eat underground roots and tubers. The pocket mice of North, Central, and South America eat grain.

Scaly-tailed squirrels These African rain forest dwellers are, apart from one species, excellent gliders. Because of their gliding membranes, they cannot run from predators and so are very aggressive if cornered.

Hans Reinhard/Bruce Coleman Limited

▶ *A southern, or least flying, squirrel coming in to land. A flying squirrel uses its long tail to steer with when gliding.*

▼ *The red squirrel of Europe and Asia lives in trees. Contrary to popular belief it does not hibernate, but it does hoard food.*

David Kirshner

▲ *European beavers are famed for their dam-building skills. They also build elaborate lodges with branches and trees, which they fell by gnawing through the trunks.*

▶ *The hoary marmot lives in colonies and has strong claws for digging burrows.*

David Kirshner

David Kirshner

Jane Burton/Bruce Coleman Limited

▲ *The European water vole (known as the water rat in England) is related to mice and rats, but has smaller eyes, a blunter snout, and a shorter tail.*

Mouse-like Rodents

Mouse-like rodents are found all over the world. They have successfully adapted to nearly all types of habitat and account for more than a quarter of all mammal species.

Rats and mice Rats and mice are well known for having many babies. Many species have gestation periods of 20 to 30 days. Litters of 3 to 7 young are born and the parents breed again immediately. Typically, the young are born without fur and with their eyes closed. But within a few months the young themselves are ready to breed.

Africa is home to 51 species of rats and mice that are found nowhere else in the world.

Voles and lemmings Most of the 121 species of this subfamily are quite small, weighing less than 3 ounces

▲ *The black, or ship, rat spread to most parts of the world as a stowaway on ships.*

Rodents running rampant

Many species of mouse and rat cause havoc to crops and stored grain. In Australia, where the house mouse was introduced, populations build to unbelievable levels. One farmer recorded 28,000 dead mice on his veranda after one night's effort to poison them and 70,000 in a wheat yard in one afternoon. In the Pacific Basin and Southeast Asia three species of rat do considerable damage to sugar cane, coconuts, oil palm, and rice.

During the Middle Ages the plague, or Black Death, claimed more human lives than any other epidemic. It was transmitted — via fleas, dirt, and urine — by the black rat.

(100 g). These rodents are mainly surface-dwellers and burrowers of northern regions.

Voles and lemmings are active throughout the winter, surviving beneath the snow in elaborate tunnel systems.

Subterranean rats Eastern Europe, Africa, and Asia are hosts to twenty-two species of subterranean (underground) rat. These rats live in burrows and eat roots and bulbs. The species that have adapted best to living underground are the eight species of blind mole-rats. They have no external ears, no tail, and eyes that are permanently beneath the skin.

Desert dwellers Within this group are hamsters, gerbils, and jerboas. They are confined to Asia and Africa, and the hamster also has a limited range in Europe. Jerboas are different from hamsters and gerbils because they have extended back legs that allow them to move quickly over very long distances. One animal has been recorded covering 7½ miles (12 km) in one night.

Most gerbils and jerboas live in deserts or very arid areas. During the day they sleep in a deep burrow, with the entrance blocked to keep it moist. They do not need to drink, but get sufficient water from their diet of seeds.

Dormice Dormice live in parts of Africa, Europe, Asia, Arabia, and Japan. Most species eat fruits, nuts, seeds, and buds. Dormice can be very vocal: they twitter, shriek, click, growl, and whistle. They probably do this when mating or protecting their territory.

Cavy-like Rodents

This group of rodents gets its name from the South American guinea pig, or cavy. Mammals in this group share similar jaw muscles, and most have a sturdy body, large head, slender limbs, and a short tail.

Porcupines of the New World American porcupines have shorter protective spines than their counterparts in the

Old World. They eat plants and are unaggressive and slow-moving. They spend a lot of time in the trees — especially the tree porcupines and prehensile-tailed porcupines. Muscles in the porcupine's skin erect the quills when a porcupine is in danger. Small barbs on the quills ensure they stick in an attacker's flesh.

Porcupines of the Old World Old World porcupines live in warmer regions of Africa, Asia, and Europe. The different species come in a variety of forms and shapes. Three species have long tails. African and Asian brush-tail porcupines have quills that can be rattled as a warning to predators. Some short-tail species have very long quills. All are vegetarian and prefer roots, bulbs, and fruit.

Spiny rats There are fifty-five species of spiny rat. Most of these have hard, lance-shaped hairs scattered through their fur. Although they are not closely related to porcupines, the spiny rats suggest how quills may have evolved from ordinary hairs.

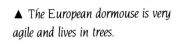

NHPA/Australasian Nature Transparencies

▲ *The European dormouse is very agile and lives in trees.*

▼ *The golden agouti of South America is a sociable animal that shares a common burrow system. It feeds mainly on fruit, sitting on its hindlimbs holding food in its forelimbs.*

David Kirshner

▼ *When the crested porcupine, an Old World species, is threatened, it erects its quills and rattles them. It then rushes backward or to the side, attempting to drive the quills into its attacker.*

David Kirshner

63

Hans Reinhard/Bruce Coleman Limited

Hans Reinhard/Bruce Coleman Limited

▲ *The Arctic, or alpine, hare has a brown or gray summer coat (left) which changes to white in winter (right) to conceal it from predators such as the Arctic fox and snowy owl. The tips of its ears remain black — a feature of all hares.*

▼ *Because they do not hibernate, pikas store leaves and grass in summer to eat, as hay, in winter. The Russians call them "haystack makers".*

Martin W Grosnick/Ardea London

Hares, Rabbits, and Pikas

Hares, rabbits, and pikas have an almost worldwide distribution, either naturally occurring or because of introduction by humans. These mammals have large ears, as well as eyes set at the side of the head, which gives them a wide range of vision.

Pikas

The pika, the smallest mammal in this group, has large, rounded ears and no tail. It lives in rocky areas of western North America and northeastern Asia.

Pikas have an average body temperature of 104.2°F (40.1°C) and must hardly move during the heat of the day or they will overheat.

Hares and rabbits

Rabbits are considered pests in many parts of the world. European rabbits live in organized groups controlled by fierce fighting. Rabbits and hares are preyed upon by many carnivorous animals and birds of prey. When they sense danger, they thump the ground with their hind feet and flash their white tails as they run. Rabbits are renowned for their breeding habits. One doe (female) can produce as many as 30 young per year. The young, in turn, are ready to breed at three and a half months.

The spectacular chasing and "boxing matches" of mating brown hares has given rise to the phrase "mad as a March hare."

Elephant Shrews

Elephant shrews are unrelated to either elephants or shrews. They are so named because the long, flexible snout looks rather like an elephant's trunk. These African mammals can jump and run at impressive speeds.

Eating and being eaten

Elephant shrews have varied diets. They eat ants, termites, beetles, worms, leaf litter, grubs, grasshoppers, spiders, and small lizards. Elephant shrews are in turn eaten by snakes, owls, small carnivores, and some native peoples of East Africa who hunt them with dogs.

Elephant shrews usually mate for life. Together, each pair defends a fixed territory from other elephant shrews. Males fight male intruders and females fight female intruders.

Within the territory, at least one species builds a system of trails. The male spends much of his time clearing debris from the trails, which provide escape routes from danger.

As with many mammals, the survival of elephant shrews will depend on the conservation of the areas they live in.

Jane Burton/Bruce Coleman Limited

▲ This spectacled elephant shrew is eating a cricket. Spectacled elephant shrews usually prefer ants and termites, breaking into their tunnel systems by clawing and biting.

Jen & Des Bartlett/Bruce Coleman Limited

◄ Elephant shrews have long, slender legs and can run fast or bound like miniature antelopes. Species range from mouse-size to some the size of a half-grown rabbit. They all have large eyes and long, rat-like tails.

Glossary

AMPHIBIAN: An animal that starts its life in the water and lives on land as an adult.

ANTLER: One of two hard horns on the head of a male deer and other animals.

BOUNDARY: A dividing line or limit.

BROWSE: To feed or graze the way cattle or deer do, by moving from place to place.

BURROW: A hole in the ground dug by an animal, to live and shelter in.

CARNIVORE: An animal that eats mainly meat.

COLD-BLOODED: Having a body temperature that changes as the temperature of the surrounding air or water changes.

COLONY: A group of animals of the same kind that live close together.

CRUSTACEAN: A type of animal, such as a crab or crayfish, with a hard shell instead of a skeleton.

CUD: Food that cattle, and some other animals, return from stomach to mouth to chew again.

DUNG: Waste matter from the bowels of animals.

ENVIRONMENT: The physical conditions of a place, such as weather, water, and vegetation.

EQUATOR: The imaginary circle around the Earth, halfway between the poles, where the climate is usually hot and wet.

EXTINCT: No longer existing.

FAMILY: A group of animals with many things in common.

FOSSIL: The remains of a plant or animal from long ago, preserved as rock.

GENUS: A group of species with many features in common or a single distinct species.

GESTATION PERIOD: The time it takes for the young of placental mammals and marsupials to develop inside the mother before they are born.

GLAND: A part of the body that produces a substance used in another part of the body.

GRASSLAND: An area of land where there are more native grasses growing wild than any other plants, and where there are few trees.

HERBIVORE: An animal that eats plants.

HIBERNATE: To hide away and sleep through the winter.

HORMONE: A chemical substance that is made by a gland in the body and that travels through the blood and affects other parts of the body.

INCUBATE: To supply eggs and young with heat so that they can develop.

INVERTEBRATE: An animal without a backbone.

LARVA: The young of any insect that changes its body before becoming an adult, such as a caterpillar before it becomes a moth.

LITTER: (1) A number of baby animals born to the same mother at the same time; (2) A mass of dead leaves and twigs scattered on the floor of a forest.

MAMMAL: An animal whose young feeds on its mother's milk.

MARSUPIAL: A mammal that keeps and feeds its young in a pouch.

MEMBRANE: A thin sheet or film of something.

MIGRATE: To change the place of living at regular times each year, as some rodents do.

MOLAR: A tooth found at the back of the mouth that is suited for grinding up food.

MOLLUSK: An animal with a soft body, a hard shell, and no backbone, such as a snail or an octopus.

MONOTREME: An egg-laying mammal.

MOLT: To lose or throw off old fur or skin.

NECTAR: A sweet liquid made by plants.

NOCTURNAL: Active by night.

NUTRIENT: A substance that provides the body with food and energy.

OMNIVORE: An animal that eats both animals and plants.

ORDER: A group of animal families.

PLACENTA: The organ that gives food and oxygen to a baby in its mother's womb.

PRAIRIE: A flat, grassy plain with no trees, especially in America or Canada.

PRIMITIVE: Being the earliest in existence.

RAIN FOREST: Thick forest in moderately warm to very hot areas that have heavy rainfall and high humidity.

RANGE: A large area of land where a kind of animal, or group of animals, normally lives.

REPTILE: An animal that is covered in scales, breathes air through lungs, and whose body heat changes as the temperature of the air or water changes.

SCALE: One of the thin, flat, fingernail-like plates that form the covering of fish and some other animals.

SPECIES: The basic category that scientists use to classify animals.

SUCKLE: To nurse, or feed milk, from the breasts or teats.

TERRITORY: Land thought of as belonging to a particular animal or group of animals.

TUNDRA: A treeless Arctic plain where mosses, lichens, and dwarf plants grow.

TUSK: The very long tooth, usually one of a pair, that animals such as elephants and wild boars have.

VERTEBRATE: An animal with a backbone.

WARM-BLOODED: Being able to maintain a constant body temperature, within certain limits.

How Scientists Group Mammals

The world has a lot more mammals than we've shown you here. Some of the larger ones appear in the companion volume, The Sierra Club Book of Great Mammals. Did you know there are about 4,300 kinds of mammals, both large and small?

To keep track of all these creatures, scientists have a special way of grouping them using Latin names. These different groups are called species, genus, family, order, and class. For example, the red wolf is known as the species Canis rufus, which belongs to the genus Canis, which belongs to the family Canidae, which belongs to the order Carnivora. This way, every single type of animal on Earth can be identified by its Latin name.

All mammals belong to the "class" called Mammalia. Below is a list of the orders in the Mammalia class. Some examples are listed for each order.

Monotremata
Spiny anteaters (echidnas), platypuses

Marsupialia
Opossums, wombats, koalas, kangaroos

Edentata
Anteaters, sloths, armadillos

Insectivora
Shrews, moles, hedgehogs

Scandentia
Tree shrews

Dermoptera
Flying lemurs

Chiroptera
Bats

Primates
Monkeys, apes, humans

Carnivora
Dogs, bears, cats, seals

Cetacea
Whales, dolphins

Sirenia
Dugongs, manatees

Proboscidea
Elephants

Perissodactyla
Horses, tapirs, rhinoceroses

Hyracoidea
Hyraxes

Tubulidentata
Aardvarks

Artiodactyla
Pigs, hippopotamuses, camels, deer, cattle

Pholidota
Pangolins

Rodentia
Beavers, squirrels, mice, rats, porcupines

Lagomorpha
Pikas, rabbits

Macroscelidea
Elephant shrews

Index